THE INUIT

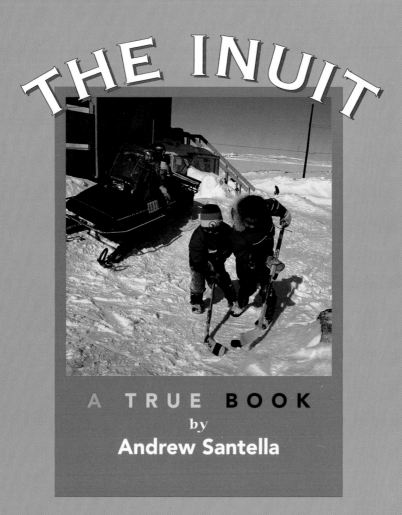

A TRUE BOOK

by

Andrew Santella

Children's Press®

A Division of Grolier Publishing

New York   London   Hong Kong   Sydney
Danbury, Connecticut

An Inuit girl
and her puppy

Reading Consultants
Linda Cornwell
*Coordinator of School Quality
and Professional Improvement
Indiana State Teachers
Association*

Lane Roy Gauthier
*Associate Professor of
Education
University of Houston*

The photograph on the cover
shows an Inuit family at their
hunting camp in Labrador,
Canada. The photograph
on the title page shows Inuit
children playing hockey
in Canada.

Visit Children's Press® on
the Internet at:
http://publishing.grolier.com

Library of Congress Cataloging-in-Publication Data

Santella, Andrew.
The Inuit / by Andrew Santella.
    p. cm.— (A True book)
    Includes bibliographical references and index.
    ISBN 0-516-22217-1 (lib.bdg.)   0-516-27319-1(pbk.)
    Inuit—History—Juvenile literature. 2. Inuit—Social life and customs—
Juvenile literature. [1. Inuit. 2. Eskimos.] I. Title. II. "True book" series.

E99.E7 S319 2001
971.9004'9712—dc21   00-024014

GROLIER
PUBLISHING

Contents

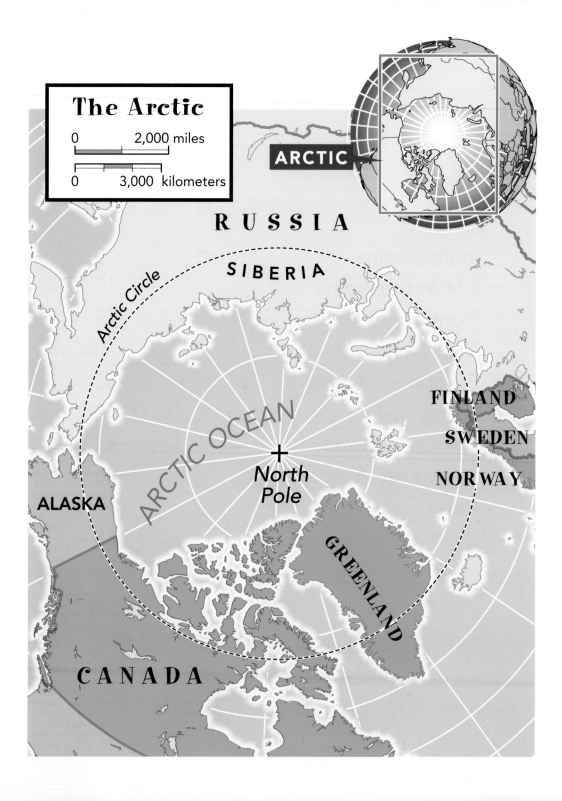

The Arctic

0   2,000 miles

0   3,000 kilometers

ARCTIC

RUSSIA

SIBERIA

Arctic Circle

FINLAND

SWEDEN

NORWAY

ARCTIC OCEAN

+ North Pole

ALASKA

GREENLAND

CANADA

Inuit Origins

The Inuit (EE-neu-eet) are a group of people that live in the lands of the far north. This area of land and water that surrounds the North Pole is called the Arctic.

There are about 100,000 Inuit in the world. About 43,000 Inuit live in Alaska and

The village of Grise Fjord in Canada

another 20,000 live in Canada, while others live in Greenland and Siberia. Some Inuit live very close to the North Pole. One Canadian Inuit village, called Grise Fjord (FYORD), is just 500 miles (805 km) from the North Pole.

The Inuit's ancestors came to North America from Asia. No one knows exactly why or when they moved. After leaving Asia, they traveled from place to place in search of food and better living conditions. They probably followed the migrating animals they hunted, such as bison and mastodons (MAS-tuh-dons).

These people used to be called Eskimos, but now they prefer the name "Inuit."

Mastodons were elephant-like animals that lived thousands of years ago.

Inuit used to be called Eskimos, a name that comes from the Algonquian (al-GON-kwee-en) family of Indian languages. The Inuit would rather not be called Eskimos. They prefer the name "Inuit," which in their own language means "the real people."

Life in the Arctic

The Arctic is one of the coldest places in the world. Ice and snow cover the ground for most of the year. In some places, the ground is always frozen. In the winter, temperatures can fall as low as −85 degrees Fahrenheit (−65 degrees Celsius). The Inuit

Much of the Arctic is usually covered with ice and snow.

have made this bitterly cold place their home by adapting to the environment. Their struggle to survive has shaped their entire way of life.

In the autumn, the ground becomes very colorful where many living things grow.

Some plants, animals, and other living things manage to survive in this cold climate. Many kinds of wildflowers and grasses thrive in the summer sunshine. Lichens grow thick on rocks and trees, and mosses cover the ground.

Musk-ox (top) and polar bears (bottom) live in the Arctic.

Wolves, foxes, musk-oxen, caribou, hares, and weasels all live in the Arctic. Many polar bears also live there. Geese and ducks arrive in the spring and then fly south in the fall.

A mother seal peaks out of the water to check on her baby seal. A baby seal is called a pup.

Eagles and owls hunt mice in the summer. Salmon and other fish live in the rivers and lakes. Seals and walruses make their homes on large pieces of drifting ice in the ocean. There are even insects such as bees, butterflies, and grasshoppers.

The Arctic goes through long periods of daylight and long periods of darkness. From October to February, the Arctic is always dark. This is because the North Pole is tilted away from the sun during the winter months. In the summer, the Arctic is always light—even at night. This is because the North Pole is tilted toward the sun during the summer. That's why the Arctic is called the "Land of the Midnight Sun."

Even in the harsh conditions of the far north, the Inuit like to play games. One game is called sky tossing. One person stands in the middle of a large animal skin, surrounded by a circle of people.

Tossing

All together, the circle of people grab the edge of the animal skin and yank it. The skin snaps up in the middle and the person standing there pops up in the air—just as if he or she were on a trampoline.

Hunting

For centuries, the Inuit hunted animals for survival. They mainly ate meat and fish. Inuit killed only the animals they needed and wasted nothing.

They found uses for every part of the animals. Inuit women sewed animal skins into clothing and blankets.

The Inuit have used many types of hunting weapons throughout the years (left). Inuit women hold up the beautiful blanket they made from sealskin (below).

Inuit burned animal fat in special lamps to light their homes. They sharpened animal bones and teeth into hunting and fishing tools. By carefully using all parts of the animals, the Inuit were able to live for a long time on just one animal. Fifteen families could survive for a year on the meat, blubber, and oil of one whale.

On the water, Inuit hunted in kayaks (KIE-aks). Kayaks are one-person boats made of bone or wood and covered

The Inuit still use kayaks (top) and dogsleds (bottom) for many purposes, including transportation and sports.

with sealskin. Inuit hunted for whales in umiaks (OO-me-aks)— eight-person boats also made of animal skins. On land, Inuit traveled in dogsleds made of animal

21

bones and skin. The dogsleds slid on runners that were glazed with ice to make them more slippery. Teams of eight to sixteen dogs pulled them.

Inuit used knives, spears, and harpoons to hunt. In Alaska, they threw poison-tipped spears at whales. When they hit a whale, they had no way of getting it out of the ocean. They hoped the animal would drift back to shore. Inuit would eat the muktuk—the inner layer of whale skin—raw.

These are traditional Inuit hunting weapons.

In eastern Canada, Inuit learned to use harpoons to hunt whales, seals, and other sea animals. Inuit harpoons had three parts. The head was

An Inuit man fixes the line on his harpoon.

made of a sharpened walrus tusk or a caribou's antler. It was attached to a short rod, usually made of ivory. This rod was fastened to a 6-foot-long (2-meter) handle, made of bone or wood. With the harpoon, they could keep hold of their prey and drag it ashore.

To become better hunters, Inuit learned the habits of the animals they hunted. Inuit knew that seals must keep air holes open in the ice all through winter because they have to come up for air every twenty minutes. The Inuit looked for these holes and then waited for the seals to appear. Then the Inuit tried to harpoon the seals. The hunter held on to the harpoon with a rope and dragged the seal up onto the ice.

Hunting for land animals was even harder. Animals could easily see hunters coming over the flat land, so the Inuit had to develop hunting strategies. To hunt caribou (large deer), a group of Inuit might drive the herd into a lake. There, more

A herd of caribou in Alaska

hunters would wait in kayaks
to spear the caribou while the
animals were in the water.

Inuit Art

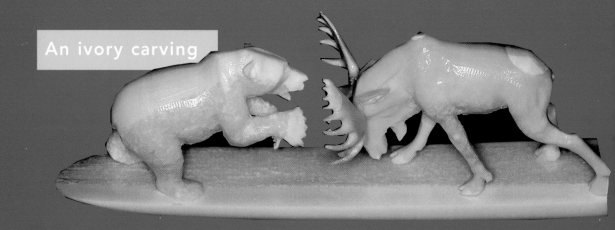

The Inuit make beautiful objects of art. They have always been skilled craftspeople. Inuit artists carve figures of bears and seals out of stone, ivory (animal tusk), and other materials. They believe that in every piece of stone,

A whale bone mask

Inuit dolls

there is a figure waiting to be carved. Today, many Inuit make their living as artists or crafts-people. In some villages, nearly half of the people are artists.

Clothing and Shelter

To keep warm, Inuit dressed in layers of loose-fitting clothing. On top of all these layers, they wore a fur parka that hung down to their knees. They also wore sealskin boots called kamiks (KA-miks) or mukluks. Some Inuit still dress this way.

An Inuit girl keeps warm in a fur parka while taking a ride with her father. Some traditional Inuit clothes are very colorful.

Inuit women made clothes from the skins of seals, caribou, bears, foxes, and other animals.

They scraped the skins clean with a knife called an ulu (OO-loo). Then they chewed on the skins to make them softer.

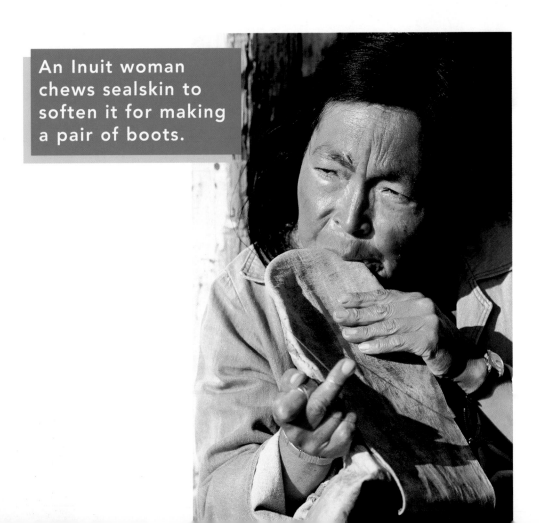

An Inuit woman chews sealskin to soften it for making a pair of boots.

Some Inuit traditionally lived in temporary shelters called igloos. An igloo is made of blocks of hard-packed snow. Inuit stacked the blocks in smaller and smaller circles until they formed a dome. An Inuit family could build an

igloo in just a few hours. All they needed was snow and a knife. To enter an igloo, Inuit had to crawl through a tunnel. Inside, there was no furniture. The Inuit slept and sat on platforms made of snow and ice.

Europeans Arrive

The Inuit first met outsiders about one thousand years ago when Vikings traveled to Greenland and Canada. The Vikings were sailors from the European countries of Norway and Denmark. By the 1800s, merchants and missionaries from Great Britain, France,

Russia, Spain, and the United States also arrived.

Over the years, the outsiders began to change the Inuit way of life. The Europeans brought diseases that killed many Inuit. The Canadian government tried to convince Inuit to live in villages, instead of moving from place to place to hunt. Inuit were urged to speak English, instead of their own language, Inuktitut (i-NOOK-tuh-toot). The U.S. government even tried to teach some Inuit to herd reindeer.

The Inuit way of life has changed throughout the years.

In the 1970s, Inuit in Canada began to gain more control over their own lives. They hoped to form a territory in Canada that they could run themselves. In 1993, the

A village in the new territory of Nunavut

Canadian government finally agreed. In 1999, the territory of Nunavut (NOO-na-voot) was created in northern Canada. Nunavut means "our land" in Inuktitut. Inuktitut is the official language of Nunavut.

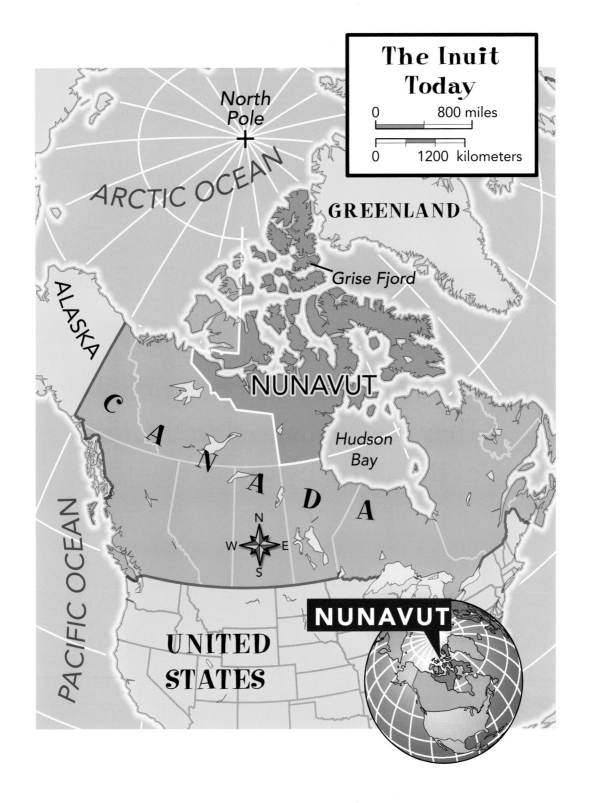

The Inuit Today

| 0 | 800 miles |
| 0 | 1200 kilometers |

North Pole

ARCTIC OCEAN

GREENLAND

ALASKA

Grise Fjord

NUNAVUT

Hudson Bay

C A N A D A

N
W · E
S

PACIFIC OCEAN

UNITED STATES

NUNAVUT

Living Today

Today, most Inuit live in villages of 300 to 1,500 people. They are connected to the rest of the world by the Internet, television, and regular airplane flights to cities in southern Canada.

Inuit life has changed a great deal. Motorboats have

Inuit children play video games (left) and go to school (below).

replaced kayaks. Snowmobiles have replaced dogsleds. Inuit children now attend school.

Inuit can buy clothing in stores instead of making it themselves. They often eat food imported from other parts of the world. At the same time, they are also trying to keep alive their language and their traditions. They eat "country food," which is meat and fish prepared according to Inuit traditions. Many still keep dog teams for racing. The Inuit are changing along with the world around them.

Inuit can buy what they need at the local store (left), but they also continue to make many things in the traditional way (below).

To Find Out More

Here are some additional resources to help you learn more about the Inuits:

 **Books**

Bonvillain, Nancy. **The Inuit.** Chelsea House, 1995.

Hancock, Lyn. **Nunavut.** Lerner Publications, 1997.

Harper, Judith E. **Inuits.** Smart Apple Media, 1999.

Lassieur, Allison. **The Inuit.** Bridgestone Books, 2000.

Siska, Heather Smith. **People of the Ice.** Firefly Books, 1995.

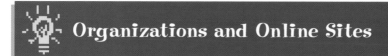

Organizations and Online Sites

Department of Indian Affairs and Northern Development
Ottawa, Ontario
Canada
K1A 0H4
http://www.inac.gc.ca/pubs/ information/info16.html

This site is about the culture of the Inuit in Canada.

Inuit Culture
http://www.arctic-travel.com/ chapters/incultpage.html

This site displays information about the Inuit way of life.

Native American History Navigator
http://www.ilt.columbia.edu/ k12/naha/nanav.html

This site has links to maps and information on history of the Inuit and American Indians.

Nunavut
http://www.nunavut.com

This site is an introduction to Canada's newest territory, Nunavut.

Important Words

Inuktitut the official language of the Inuit

kayak a one-person boat made of bone or wood and covered with sealskin

merchants people who buy and sell things to make a profit

missionaries people who travel to spread their religion

mukluks Inuit boots made from sealskin; also known as kamiks

muktuk the inner layer of whale skin

territory an area of land that has its own government

umiak a boat made of animal skin that holds eight people

46

Index

Meet the Author

Andrew Santella lives in Chicago, Illinois. He is a graduate of Loyola University, where he studied American literature. He writes for a wide variety of newspapers and magazines, including *The New York Times Book Review* and *GQ*. He is also the author of several books for young people, including the following Children's Press titles: *The Battle of the Alamo*, *The Capitol*, and *The Chisholm Trail*.